Mitsubishi TD05/TD06 16G, 18G, and 20G:
Turbo Rebuild Guide and Shop Manual

Brian Smothers

Table of Contents

Special Note

This book is not written, authorized, or produced in collaboration with Mitsubishi Heavy Industries, Cummins, Cummins Turbo Technologies, or Chrysler Group LLC. This book and all of its content is produced by Brian Smothers, an independent turbocharger rebuilder.

Background

There are a number of guides to repairing a turbocharger found online. None of these guides mention checking any specs at all or re machining anything. Some of them involve using vice grips. None of these guides are written by a turbocharger professional, they are just educated guesses.

We have attempted to create a guide that addresses the shortcomings of other guides found online, and we have attempted to create a guide that fills the gaps that many diesel mechanics may have in turbocharger knowledge.

Please note, this guide is a general guide that also contains specific information regarding the TD05/6 family turbocharger manufactured by Mitsubishi Heavy Industries: the specific information regarding tolerances and dimensions ONLY relates to this specific turbo. Torque settings, machining tolerances, etc., should NOT be generalized from this guide to cover any turbocharger other than the TD05/6 family family of turbos. SO:

Rebuilding the Mitsubishi TD05/6 family turbocharger is relatively simple and easy to do under the following conditions

- Your TD05/6 family turbocharger does not have damage to the wheels
- Your TD05/6 family turbocharger does not have damage to the turbine shaft
- Your TD05/6 family turbocharger does not have damage to the bearing housing
- Your TD05/6 family turbocharger does not have damage to the compressor or turbine housing

If your TD05/6 family turbocharger had damage to these above listed parts, these parts must be replaced. Additionally, there are published wear tolerances for the TD05/6 family of turbochargers, and once these tolerances are exceeded, the TD05/6 family turbocharger must be brought back into spec using oversized bearings and rebalancing of components and or the entire assembly.

The only time a TD05/6 family turbocharger may be rebuilt and not rebalanced is if there is no measurable wear or if no parts have been replaced. If a TD05/6 family turbocharger has had its bearings and seals replaced and NO other major parts have been repaired, it is still recommended that the entire rotating assembly be rebalanced.

Rebuilding a TD05/6 family turbocharger is something done with no warranty implied or granted, and the reader of this file assumes all liability and risk when attempting a rebuild of a TD05/6 family turbocharger. Any attempted rebuild of a TD05/6 family turbocharger by anyone but a authorized Mitsubishi Turbocharger service center may end in failure. This guide is for entertainment purposes only and should not be used or read by anyone ever for any reason.

Special Note:

There are a number of so-called Mitsubishi TD05/6 turbos for sale online that are very Chinese. Many of these turbochargers are NOT Mitsubishi spec TD05/6 family replicas, they are something else. Their parts are NOT compatible with TD05/6 family parts because they are not the same size. The only way to know what you have is to measure your turbine shaft and bearing housing bore. These specs are found in the "inspection" section of this guide.

Tools Needed

Now that you know not to do this, here are the tools you will need:

- Socket set (typically metric, but many bolts are ½ SAE), 12 point
- Wrench set, 12 point
- Torque wrenches (depending on the size of the turbo, you may need a wrench that reads as low as 1n/m)
- Small flat screwdriver
- Allen keys
- Torx screwdrivers or sockets
- Propane Torch
- Penetrating oil
- Internal snap ring pliers, large and small
- Steel hammer (3 lb handheld sledge is best, but a framing hammer will do in a pinch)
- Steel punch
- Dental Picks
- 1500 or greater grit sandpaper
- Soft face hammer
- Motor oil
- V blocks
- Dial caliper
- Bore gage
- Dawn dish soap
- Electric Pencil
- Dremel Tool
- Fire extinguisher

Recommended, but not needed
- Wooden table
- Shop vice
- WCB30 rotor balancer
- Steel straight edge
- Oil can for motor oil

Attachments

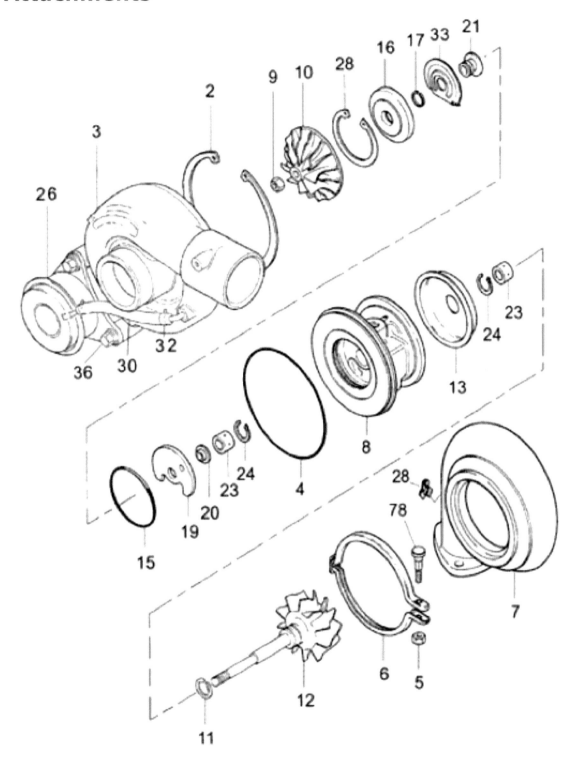

Illustration 1: Mitsubishi Heavy Industries TD05/6 Family Turbocharger (parts common)

Table 1: Part Numbers Covered by this Guide

All Mitsubishi TD05, TD05h, TD06, TD06h, TD06R, TD05R, EVOIII, and hybrid turbochargers that utilize a Mitsubishi TD05/6 bearing system

49178-00200	49178-00980	49178-02115	49178-03130	49178-91340
49178-00210	49178-00990	49178-02120	49178-03133	49178-91400
49178-00300	49178-01000	49178-02121	49178-03140	49178-91450
49178-00310	49178-01010	49178-02122	49178-03150	49178-91560
49178-00340	49178-01030	49178-02123	49178-03160	49378-00211
49178-00410	49178-01100	49178-02125	49178-03200	49378-01500
49178-00500	49178-01200	49178-02126	49178-03530	49378-01510
49178-00510	49178-01340	49178-02130	49178-04000	49378-01520
49178-00520	49178-01400	49178-02135	49178-04200	49378-01530
49178-00530	49178-01410	49178-02136	49178-04300	49378-01540
49178-00540	49178-01411	49178-02140	49178-04310	49378-01550
49178-00550	49178-01420	49178-02145	49178-04320	49378-01560
49178-00590	49178-01450	49178-02150	49178-04330	49378-01570
49178-00595	49178-01460	49178-02155	49178-04340	49378-01571
49178-00600	49178-01470	49178-02160	49178-04400	49378-01580
49178-00610	49178-01500	49178-02170	49178-04410	49378-01581
49178-00620	49178-01510	49178-02180	49178-04500	49179-00100
49178-00630	49178-01520	49178-02190	49178-04510	49179-00110
49178-00640	49178-01540	49178-02200	49178-05000	49179-00120
49178-00650	49178-01550	49178-02210	49178-05010	49179-00130
49178-00660	49178-01560	49178-02300	49178-05020	49179-00150
49178-00670	49178-01570	49178-02305	49178-05040	49179-00160
49178-00680	49178-01580	49178-02310	49178-05050	49179-00180
49178-00690	49178-01590	49178-02315	49178-05060	49179-00191
49178-00700	49178-01600	49178-02320	49178-05070	49179-00200
49178-00800	49178-01700	49178-02325	49178-05080	49179-00210
49178-00810	49178-01710	49178-02330	49178-05090	49179-00220
49178-00820	49178-01730	49178-02335	49178-05100	49179-00230
49178-00830	49178-01740	49178-02340	49178-05200	49179-00240
49178-00840	49178-01750	49178-02350	49178-05530	49179-00251
49178-00870	49178-01760	49178-02380	49178-06200	49179-00252
49178-00880	49178-01900	49178-02385	49178-06290	49179-00253
49178-00890	49178-02000	49178-02400	49178-06300	49179-00254
49178-00900	49178-02001	49178-02500	49178-06310	49179-00260
49178-00910	49178-02003	49178-03000	49178-06380	49179-00261
49178-00930	49178-02010	49178-03010	49178-06390	49179-00270
49178-00940	49178-02100	49178-03122	49178-07200	49179-00280
49178-00970	49178-02110	49178-03123	49178-91200	49179-00290

49179-00300	49179-01040	49179-05000
49179-00400	49179-01050	49179-06000
49179-00440	49179-01060	
49179-00450	49179-01070	
49179-00451	49179-01080	
49179-00460	49179-01090	
49179-00490	49179-01100	
49179-00510	49179-01120	
49179-00520	49179-01130	
49179-00530	49179-01140	
49179-00541	49179-01150	
49179-00600	49179-01160	
49179-00610	49179-01170	
49179-00620	49179-01180	
49179-00630	49179-01190	
49179-00640	49179-01200	
49179-00650	49179-01210	
49179-00660	49179-01220	
49179-00670	49179-01230	
49179-00680	49179-02000	
49179-00690	49179-02100	
49179-00700	49179-02110	
49179-00800	49179-02120	
49179-00810	49179-02200	
49179-00820	49179-02210	
49179-00830	49179-02220	
49179-00840	49179-02230	
49179-00850	49179-02240	
49179-00860	49179-02250	
49179-00870	49179-02260	
49179-00880	49179-02270	
49179-00890	49179-02280	
49179-00910	49179-02300	
49179-00920	49179-02400	
49179-01000	49179-02410	
49179-01010	49179-03000	
49179-01020	49179-04000	
49179-01030	49179-04100	

Glossary of Terms

Bearing Housing: The cast iron bearing housing is part of the CHRA, and it holds the bearing system and contains oil and coolant passages (#8 in illustration above)

Backplate: The portion of a turbocharger that connects to the compressor housing. The backplate also contains the turbocharger's compressor-side piston ring and thrust spacer or oil slinger

Billet Wheel: The common term for a compressor wheel that has been manufactured from a single piece of billet aluminum using a five axis CNC mill. Contrary to popular belief, billet compressor wheels were not developed as a weight saving measure, they were designed in order to gain strength and eliminate flaws created by the casting process traditionally used to create compressor wheels. Most billet wheels are heavier, but stronger, than cast aluminum compressor wheels

Blowoff Valve (BOV): (not pictured) All gasoline, and almost no diesel, engines have blowoff valves. Many times, a turbocharger will have an integrated blowoff valve on the compressor cover. The BOV opens when the engine's throttle plate closes, creating backpressure that pushes against the turbocharger's compressor wheel. This backpressure, when the BOV opens, is vented away from the turbocharger, allowing the turbocharger to spin freely.

CHRA: Center Housing Rotating Assembly, consisting of the bearing housing, bearings and seals, compressor wheel, and turbine wheel and shaft. The CHRA is a modular assembly that can be serviced or replaced as a unit

Coking: The condition created when engine oil has broken down due to heat and or an extended service life. Coked oil turns into a semi solid and coats all of the internal parts of a turbocharger, and semi-sold coked oil tends to obstruct a turbocharger's oil passages, including the small holes in the journal bearing and thrust bearings

Compressor Cover: A piece of machined cast aluminum that attaches to the bearing housing and covers the compressor wheel. Commonly called a snail or shroud (#3 in illustration above)

Compressor Wheel: Made of cast aluminum or CNC machined titanium aluminum alloys, the compressor wheel is driven by the turbine wheel in order to compress air. This compression of air increases the concentration of oxygen in an internal combustion engine's fuel air mixture, adding power to the combustion of that mixture (#10 in illustration above)

Compressor Wheel Hub: The center of the compressor wheel that extends upward from the extreme inside of the compressor wheel blades. The turbocharger's compressor wheel is secured to the turbine shaft by tightening the shaft nut against the compressor wheel hub

Journal Bearing: Sometimes called a bushing, the journal bearing rides on two layers of thin pressurized oil. The journal bearing sits in the bearing housing and contains the turbine shaft (#23 in illustration above)

Oil Slinger: On older Garrett turbochargers, the thrust collar and thrust spacer are contained in this part. The oil slinger has machined holes that throw or sling the oil inside of a turbocharger

Piston Ring: A piston ring is a gapped high temperature steel ring that is found on a turbocharger's thrust collar or oil flinger, depending on the application, and on a turbocharger's turbine shaft. Some older turbochargers do not have a compressor side piston ring because they are designed to work with carburetors. Some larger turbochargers have more than one piston ring sealing each end of the turbocharger. Piston rings are the turbocharger's seal system, but contrary to popular opinion, a turbocharger's seals typically do not go out. When a turbocharger smokes due to oil loss and is said to have bad seals, worn seal plates or backplates are commonly at fault, not piston rings (#17 and #11 in illustration above)

Seal Plate: A turbocharger's seal plate is a wear item/serviceable part that contains a turbocharger's thrust collar and compressor side piston ring. Unlike a backplate, a seal plate does not attach to a turbocharger's compressor housing (#16 in illustration above)

TD05/6 Family Turbocharger: A turbocharger with td05 or 6 in its name. All td05/6 turbochargers share a common turbine shaft width, bearing housing bore, journal and thrust bearing size, and distance between journals. The common difference between models of td05/6 turbochargers is found in the size of the turbine and compressor wheels and compressor housing and turbine housing sizes.

Thrust Bearing: The turbocharger's thrust bearing is designed to take the thrust load generated by normal operation. Many times, a turbocharger that operates under normal engine conditions and has plenty of clean oil will only have a worn thrust bearing. Turbochargers can operate for many hours with worn thrust bearings (#19 in illustration above)

Thrust Collar: The thrust collar sits between the journal bearings and the thrust bearing (#20 in illustration above)

Thrust Spacer: The thrust spacer goes through the backplate/seal plate and contains the compressor side piston ring. It also is attached directly to the back of the compressor wheel (#21 in illustration above)

Turbine Housing: A piece of machined cast iron that attaches typically to an engine's exhaust manifold and covers the turbocharger's turbine wheel, routing exhaust gasses over the turbine wheel. (part number 7 above

Turbine Shaft: The turbine shaft is usually friction welded to the back of the turbine wheel. The turbine shaft of a turbocharger rides in a thin layer of pressurized oil inside of the journal bearings and thrust hardware and is connected to the compressor wheel (contained in #12 in illustration above)

Turbine Wheel: The turbine wheel is made of light high temperature Inconel. The turbine wheel is shrouded in the turbine housing and driven by exhaust gasses. A turbine wheel spins on a turbine shaft at speeds approaching 200,000 RPM in automotive applications using the heat of combustion generated as a byproduct in internal combustion engines (#12 in illustration above)

Turbocharger: An exhaust driven supercharger consisting of a turbine wheel and a compressor wheel connected by a common shaft

Wastegate Actuator: A small metal cylinder attached to a turbocharger that opens and closes a small door on the turbocharger's turbine housing. The opening of the flapper door diverts exhaust gasses away from the turbine wheel, slowing the rotating assembly (#26 in illustration above)

Disassembly

22

Before attempting to break down your turbocharger, remove all oil and coolant lines and fittings. This will make it easier to handle and work on your turbocharger. It is recommended that you take pictures before taking anything apart.

Turbochargers are made up of four main components. A turbocharger's rotating parts make up the center cartridge, which contains the turbine wheel, compressor wheel, bearings, and bearing housing. This center housing is typically referred to by its acronym, CHRA, which stands for center housing rotating assembly. A turbocharger's CHRA is held together on the compressor side of the turbocharger by a shaft nut, which connects to the turbo's turbine shaft (see image 2).

Image 2: Typical Center Housing Rotating Assembly (CHRA)

The turbocharger's CHRA has two covers, or shrouds, one on each end. On the hot side of the turbocharger, covering the CHRA's turbine wheel is the turbine housing (see image 3). The turbine housing is typically connected to an engine's exhaust manifold. On the other side of the turbocharger is the aluminum compressor cover, which covers the CHRA's compressor wheel (see image 4). On some, but not all, turbochargers, there is a steel cylinder with an arm that connects it to one or both shrouds of the turbocharger. This is the wastegate actuator (see image 5).

The first step in taking apart your turbocharger is to remove the wastegate actuator, if equipped. Again, take pictures before you take any piece off your turbocharger or before you take a major component apart.

The wastegate actuator is held on by bolts and usually a e clip or a pin. Remove the pin and the bolts and take the actuator off the turbo. Set the actuator aside.

Image 3: Typical Turbine Housing

Image 4: Typical Compressor Housing

Image 5: Typical Wastegate Actuator

The second step depends on your preferences. Many turbochargers do not have any locating pins or any markings that hold the parts in correct relation to each other. As you may notice, the compressor cover of the turbocharger attaches to the intercooler piping in a certain way, and if that compressor cover is 180 degrees off, or even ten degrees off, it will be difficult to attach your piping. Once you take the compressor cover off the CHRA, you have no way of knowing where to put it back so that the orientation of the air outlet, oil holes, etc. are the same. So, the way we recommend that you mark the compressor cover and turbine housing is with a Dremel tool.

Before you take anything else apart, score a mark on the turbine housing with your Dremel tool that lines up with the center of the CHRA's oil drain flange. Do the same with the turbocharger's compressor cover. Make sure the marks are deep enough to survive any cleaning of the housings. Take pictures of where the marks are oriented to the CHRA.

Now that you have marked the turbine housing and compressor housing, it is time to separate the CHRA from the turbine housing. Set the turbocharger in your vice or on a table and examine how the turbine housing connects to the CHRA. Your turbine housing is connected via a V-band clamp.

After you have removed your V-band clamp or bolts, your CHRA may easily come loose from the turbine housing. If you are this lucky, and you can remove the CHRA by hand, do so. You are probably not that lucky: do not attempt to force the CHRA out with any tools at this point.

Propane torches should never be operated indoors or in poorly ventilated areas.

First, take your propane torch and heat up the area where the CHRA attaches to the turbine housing. Allow this area to cool completely, and repeat at least two more times. After the bearing housing has completely cooled, and after you are done heating the area with your torch, apply a liberal amount of penetrating oil to your cool parts. DO NOT use the penetrating oil on hot parts and DO NOT heat up the penetrating oil with your torch. It will stink and or catch on fire, and the penetrating properties of these products are lost when they are on fire.

After your parts have soaked in oil for some time, take your steel hammer and punch GENTLY tap the turbine housing, loosening the bond caused by corrosion between the CHRA and the turbine housing. Tap gently in a circular pattern so that the turbine wheel of the CHRA does not come into contact with the turbine housing.

The reason you tap the turbine housing off the bearing housing, and the reason you tap a little bit and move on is simple: if you hit the turbine housing too hard, or if you remove the turbine housing so that it comes into contact with the turbine wheel, you will probably damage the wheel, mandating replacement. Tap your punch gently and then move it, and tap it again. Work the housing off the CHRA, don't try to take it off with one move. This is the hardest part of the rebuild and this will take the longest amount of time.

Make sure that the housing is a safe distance from a floor or from a tabletop-the turbine housing has a tendency to come off and smash people in the toes, and if you are lucky and your toes are spared, the housing may bounce off your concrete floor and ruin a flange surface or even break. After you have gently separated your turbine housing from your CHRA, set the turbine housing aside.

Now you have a CHRA and a compressor housing. Set the compressor housing with the inlet facing down on a soft surface (a wood table or on a piece of wood is best) and remove the internal type snap ring, found between the back of the compressor cover and the CHRA, with your snap ring pliers. DO NOT remove the compressor cover yet-it is very very easy to damage the soft aluminum compressor wheel.

If your turbocharger has an internal type snap ring, the best way to remove this snap ring is to compress the ring with your snap ring pliers.

YOU MUST WEAR EYE PROTECTION WHEN WORKING WITH SNAP RINGS. Snap rings can come off with a great deal of force and hit you in the eyes.

You will see that there is now a gap between the back of the snap ring and the compressor cover. Take a straight screwdriver and put it between the back of the snap ring and the compressor cover and under the snap ring. Now release the pressure on the internal snap ring pliers. The snap ring should ride the screwdriver all the way out of the compressor cover.

With the V-band clamp removed, keep the turbocharger face down on a soft surface. GENTLY tap the back of the compressor housing with your soft faced hammer, moving in a circle. This is to break the seal that may exist between the compressor cover and the CHRA. Keep tapping while holding the CHRA and compressor cover down against your soft surface so that the compressor cover CAN NOT come off. You are just breaking the seal.

After the seal seems to be broken, G E N T L Y see if you can remove the compressor cover in a way that keeps the cover COMPLETELY straight in relation to the CHRA.

You do not want to remove the cover at an angle-the clearance between the compressor wheel in the CHRA and the compressor cover is extremely tight, so do not force the cover off. If needed, GENTLY tap the cover off, working in a circular pattern. DO NOT just hit the thing with your hammer as hard as you can-it will come off with patience and a gentle touch.

IF your compressor wheel looks like Swiss cheese, or if you are just replacing your cartridge, feel free to just whack the compressor cover a few good times with your soft faced hammer: the wheel is already toast, so you are not going to hurt it any more than it already is. Depending on the size of the wheel, you may only have one part of the wheel be .005-.015 grams heavier than any other part. Even slight damage to the wheels is fatal to a turbocharger.

Once you have managed to carefully remove your compressor cover, you now only have the CHRA to take apart. If you are replacing the turbo's CHRA, you do not have to take the CHRA apart. Skip to the inspection section of this guide.

If you are tearing down the CHRA, it is now time to take a look at your CHRA and the housings you have taken off. Are the wheels nicked or worn? Is there any wear visible on the housings where the wheels have come into contact with them? Are the edges of the turbocharger jagged, rough, or worn? Any wear to a turbocharger's wheels must be corrected by replacing the wheels. A rule of thumb for the housings is this: slight wear is ok (rub marks), but any wear that results in lines being carved in the housings must be corrected by replacing the housings. ANY wear to the compressor wheel is not ok. And, of course, if your turbocharger has a snapped turbine shaft, usually all of the turbochargers rotating parts and housings are ruined. A more formal and complete inspection of the CHRA's rotating parts is found later in this guide.

If you have a bench top vice, put the CHRA in the vice, but do not tighten the vice down so much that you leave tool marks on the thing. Your CHRA will have a shaft nut on the compressor side, or the compressor wheel will have an integrated nut on the end, and if you are lucky, the turbine shaft will end with a nut as well. Many turbine shafts do not have enough material that can be grabbed with a socket or wrench, and if your turbine shaft cannot be grabbed using a proper tool, you are in trouble. ANY tool marks on a turbocharger WILL throw the rotating assembly out of balance, so Vice-Grips are not an option.

Take your electric pencil or Dremel tool and make a VERY light mark down the side of the compressor shaft nut and down the side of the compressor wheel hub (see image 5b). The idea is to mark the relationship of the shaft nut to the compressor wheel so that you can line these marks back up again when you put your CHRA back together.

Image 5b: Orientation Marks on shaft nut and compressor wheel hub

After you have made your marks, put a socket or wrench on each end of the CHRA and see if you can easily loosen the shaft nut on the compressor side of the CHRA. BE CAREFUL, and DO NOT use power tools at this point: many CHRA use left handed threads, and attempts to force off shaft nuts have resulted in snapped turbine shafts. DO NOT FORCE THE NUT OFF until you have figured out if the threads are standard or reversed. Again, the point of this exercise is to figure out which way the threads go and to NOT PUT TOOL MARKS on your parts. Once you have figured out how to accomplish this, remove the shaft nut.

If your turbine wheel does not have enough material on it to grab with a wrench or socket, a good trick is to get a shop towel and use it to grab the turbine wheel and hold it so that you can loosen the shaft nut. This operation is usually a two-person effort.

IF the compressor wheel DOES NOT want to easily come off the turbine shaft at this point, DO NOT PRY IT OFF! Take your propane torch and heat the wheel up. When the wheel is still hot, it should come off the shaft. IF YOUR COMPRESSOR WHEEL DOES NOT COME OFF THE COMPRESSOR SHAFT, you have some major problems. Your wheel is stuck on the shaft because of a major turbocharger bearing failure, which creates heat. If you cannot remove your wheel without putting tool marks on it, your cartridge is ruined and is not a suitable candidate for rebuilding. You need a new CHRA.

The same goes for your turbine wheel and shaft: you should be able, with the compressor wheel removed, to take your soft faced hammer and gently tap the threaded end of the turbine shaft out of the CHRA's bearing housing with almost no force. In fact, it will be easy to knock the turbine shaft and wheel onto the floor, ruining it, so make sure you are careful to tap the turbine wheel and shaft out gently and not too far off any surfaces. If you cannot gently tap your wheel and shaft out of place, your turbocharger probably has a shaft that is bent or deflected due to bearing failure and the resulting high levels of heat. Turbochargers can spin at 200,000 (that's two hundred thousand!) RPM, so if there is an oil problem, a major failure can result, and a stuck turbine shaft is a strong message to you, the rebuilder: do not pass go, do not collect $200. Your CHRA is ruined and is not a suitable candidate for a rebuild.

After your turbine wheel has been removed, it is time to remove the seal plate. This seal plate will be held in place either by an internal snap ring. Remove the snap ring. Many times, you have to put a screwdriver under the seal plate and pry it up (see image 8).

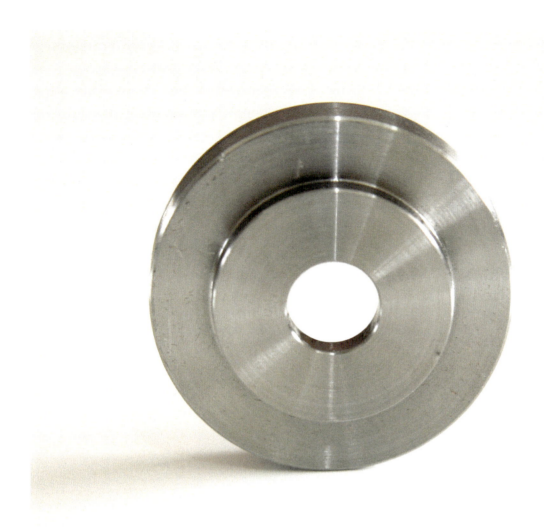

Image 8: Seal Plate

Do not worry about putting tool marks on your seal plate-it is a wear item and it will be replaced.

Behind, and going through, the backplate and sealplate will be some of your thrust hardware. Your Mitsubishi turbo will have a thrust spacer with a piston ring installed on it. This spacer and ring will be attached to your sealplate. Remove the spacer from the sealplate. Notice the gapped piston ring that fits into the sealplate: this is the 'seal' that everyone thinks is the problem with turbos. Turbo seals don't really wear out that easily, the groove that the ring sits into is usually the problem. Insufficient lubrication will wear that seal surface and allow oil to blow past the gapped ring (seal). The thrust spacer will be attached to an oil shield -you will not be able to get the shield off without removing the piston ring. Take note of how this piece goes together before disassembly (see images 9 and 9b).

Image 9: Thrust Spacer Without Piston Ring Installed

Image 9b: Thrust Spacer, seal plate, and oil deflector assembly

Behind the thrust spacer will be some kind of silicon O-ring or gasket. Take note of the gasket's location (take a picture?) and remove the gasket/o ring. In Mitsubishi turbos, the o ring is typically inside of a machined groove. Take a picture before you remove the ring.

Now you can remove the thrust bearing from the bearing housing (see image 10). Do so.

Behind the thrust bearing is the thrust collar. Remove the thrust collar. (see image 11).

Image 10: Thrust Bearing

Image 11: Thrust Collar

Now you can see the journal bearings.

Some turbochargers have journal bearings that are held in by small internal type snap rings (#64 in illustration above). Some turbochargers have no snap rings. If equipped, remove the snap ring. The journal bearing should slide out if you turn the bearing housing upside down and smack it against your hand. Another good way to get the bearing out is to reverse your small snap ring pliers so that they are set up to remove external snap rings. Expand the pliers inside of the journal bearings and pull the bearings out. If you cannot get the journal bearings out of the housing, do not pass go, do not collect $200: your journal bearings have expanded, due to a problem with lubrication, and they are now a part of the cast iron bearing housing. Your bearing housing is ruined, and your turbine shaft/wheel is probably also ruined.

On the other side of the journal bearing there is a small internal snap ring, if you are lucky, or a expanding steel ring if you are not lucky. If you have an older style turbo, there may be a steel spacer or a spring between the bearings and no clips/rings. Remove the snap rings/clips/hardware, and turn the bearing housing over and repeat the process on the other side of the bearing housing/CHRA to remove the other journal bearing. The bearing housing may have a groove and O ring on the outside of it on the compressor side. Remove the O ring.

Inspection

This is where things get technical. If you do not have the required tools and tooling to inspect EVERY surface of the rotating parts of your turbocharger, you should take this guide over to your local friendly machine shop/machinist. Turbochargers are high speed tight tolerance precision machines, and the difference between a turbo that is junk and a turbo that is a piece of garbage is typically about .007" or less, and the difference between a turbo that fails and a turbo that operates is about .012" of total tolerance stack up: this means that you cannot have any more than .012" of wear TOTAL in the rotating components or housing and expect your turbo to work correctly.

Wastegate Actuator

Your wastegate actuator should hold 5-10psi, depending on the application. This means that 5-10psi of compressed air (not 50-100 psi, that will blow the thing out) should cause the actuator's arm to go all the way out and stay out. Hook the nipple on the side of the actuator up to 5-10 psi of air and see what happens. If the arm does not move, or if the arm moves but goes back into place, replace the actuator. It is recommended that you clean and paint your actuator: they tend to rust. Keep in mind, wastegate actuators are NOT waterproof, so do not immerse the actuator in water, cleaner, etc.

Turbine and Compressor Housings

Check the turbine and compressor housings for wear. Slight contact due to rubbing from the wheels is tolerable, but contact that is caused typically by a snapped turbine shaft is intolerable. Grooves cut into either housing by the wheels mean that the housing must be replaced (see image 12).

Check the turbine housing for hairline cracks inside the housing and especially around the wastegate flapper port (if equipped). All cracks are intolerable and mandate the replacement ore repair of the housing (see image 13).

Image 12: Example of a Compressor Housing with Excessive Wear from Wheel to Housing

Contact

Image 13: Crack in Common Area (around wastegate port)

Check the flange surfaces with a steel straight edge or true steel surface: re-deck flanges if they are warped at your local machine shop.

Compressor wheel

ANY wear on a compressor wheel means that the compressor wheel must be replaced. Edge wear is the hardest to spot, and if any wear is visible inside of a compressor housing from the wheel rubbing the housing, the wheel is deadlined and must be replaced (see image 14).

Any bent fins, missing chunks, or edge wear renders a compressor wheel useless. Replace all compressor wheels with any wear.

Turbine Wheel and Shaft

First, check the turbine wheel for any wear(see image 15).

Image 14: Compressor Wheel Edge Wear

Image 15: Edge Wear from Engine Failure

Ragged edges or edge wear on a turbine wheel means that the wheel/shaft assembly must be replaced

Look at the piston ring portion of the turbine shaft, directly behind the turbine wheel (image 15a). There can be no wear in this area: grooves or lines worn into this area typically mean that this area is ruined. Replace any turbine shaft/wheel with wear in the piston portion.

Check the turbine shaft, using your v blocks and dial indicator, for runout (bent shaft). Any runout over .0025" is unacceptable. Check the turbine shaft for bluing-the turbine shaft should be shiny and silver, not blued (see image 16).

Image 15a: Piston portion of turbine shaft with piston ring installed

Image 16: Overheated Turbine Shaft with Bluing and Grooves

Check the turbine shaft for any grooves cut into it from contamination. For a TD05/6 family turbocharger, the diameter of the turbine shaft should be .2950-2953"(7.493-7.500mm). The turbine shaft **cannot** have a diameter of less than .2900" due to wear: the turbine shaft can be reground/repolished to .010" over, but oversized bearings MUST BE USED. If there is more than .010" of wear, and the turbine shaft is smaller than .2900", the turbine shaft CANNOT be reworked and it must be discarded. ANY component rework must be followed by a re balancing of the turbine wheel.

Bearing Housing

Check the bearing housing bore for wear, scratches, or rough surfaces. Using a bore gage, check the bore of the bearing housing (where the journal bearings go). The bore should be smooth and regular: any surface irregularities must be honed at a .010" increment, not to exceed .010" of rework. A TD05/6 family bearing housing should have a bore of .5118-5112"(13.00-13.010mm). If you re-hone the bearing housing to remove surface irregularities, you must use undersized bearings and re-balance the rotating assembly/CHRA.

Special Note/Seal Plate and heat shield

If your turbocharger is equipped with a Seal Plate, YOU MUST NOT re-use the seal plate. YOU MUST REPLACE THE seal plate. This is the missing fact from nearly every turbo rebuild guide found online. Do not inspect the seal plate for wear-it has wear. Discard it and replace it with a new piece. Re-use of the seal plate will result in oil pressure loss of your turbocharger, imbalance, and premature failure. Every time.

Almost every turbocharger has a heat shield attached to the bearing housing/CHRA on the turbine side (see image 16a).

Image 16a: Heat Shield

Many times, this shield is not easily seen, as it has changed shape and attached itself to the bearing housing. The heat shield must be removed-many times, a straight screwdriver and a steel hammer must be utilized in order to separate the two. If you cannot remove your heat shield, you cannot get your bearing housing clean enough, as there is always material behind the heat shield. It's your turbo, but we recommend replacing a bearing housing that has a heat shield permanently attached, as this attachment/welding is a sign of major turbocharger failure.

There is also a metal gasket between the CHRA and the turbine housing: re use this gasket.

Cleaning

It is ok to sand/media blast the turbine housing, but DO NOT use a sandblaster on a compressor housing or bearing housing. It is acceptable to media blast the turbine wheel but only if the piston portion of the wheel/shaft and the shaft are protected: the piston portion and the shaft are bearing surfaces and MUST NOT come into contact with sandblasting material. Irregular, dull, or pitted bearing surfaces from media blasting will not retain oil properly.

If the bearing housing has caked on oil/coked oil, it may be best to replace the bearing housing: coked oil may be impossible to remove from the bearing housing's oil passages and journal surfaces.

The problem with cleaning bearing housings is that they flash rust because they are cast iron. It is acceptable to put a bearing housing into a mechanical cleaner ONLY if that cleaner removes all chemical residue and only if the bearing housing is IMMEDIATELY lubricated: the journal surfaces (bore) of the bearing housing may flash rust in a minute or less, so clean the part, immediately dry it with compressed air, and immediately apply a liberal amount of oil to the bearing housing surfaces. The trickiest part to clean on the bearing housing is the piston ring groove on the turbine side: (see image 16b) the turbine

Image 16b: Bearing housing, turbine end, and piston ring groove. Note the mirror finish of the bore and the small machined groove.

shaft's piston portion has a piston ring that fits into a groove on the shaft, and that ring fits into a small groove in the bearing housing. Many times, this groove is filled completely with carbon and it may seem as though there is no groove. Every turbo has this groove. Find it and clean it!

A compressor housing can be cleaned with any chemicals or techniques, but the machined portions of the housing must remain machined: any sandblasting of the housing will change the machined surfaces into porous surfaces, and this will look bad and create turbulence. A brass brush, some degreaser, and elbow grease will clean any compressor housing.

Turbine housings are easy to clean with a sand blasting cabinet, but if you don't have one, prepare to spend an hour or more scrubbing the thing and getting filthy. It is a best practice to clean any threads on the housing with a tap or wire brush. When cleaning the turbine housing, it is important to remove any oxidation from the portion of the housing that receives the bearing housing of the CHRA: this will assure a good, easy fit. Any mechanical device (air tool, dremel) that makes this surface that receives the bearing housing of the CHRA smooth works, from emory cloth to sandpaper in a dremel. Get that surface smooth, burr free, and shiny.

You will probably never get a compressor wheel clean enough, but never use harsh chemicals or a sandblaster. Aluminum compressor wheels have a special coating that should not be removed. Just use some dish soap and a plastic scrub brush-you won't get it that clean, but don't' worry about how it looks as long as there is nothing stuck to it. Really dirty compressor wheels tend to be stained by oil, and those stains are not worth getting out if it means ruining the compressor wheel. Do not media blast the compressor wheel.

The turbine wheel is very tricky to get clean-many shops will mask the turbine shaft and piston portion of the shaft and media blast the wheel itself. You can do this, too, but keep in mind, if ANY media material hits the turbine shaft or piston portion of the shaft, that shaft is ruined. If your turbine shaft is blued due to heat, do not try to clean the bluing off: the turbine shaft must be replaced. The same goes for grooves cut into the shaft by contaminants-the only way to get these grooves out is to micropolish them (see "inspection" section above). If your turbine shaft and piston portion of the turbine shaft has coked oil or any varnish-like material, you can polish this material off using your 1500 or greater grit sandpaper. The shaft and piston portion of the turbine shaft must have a mirror finish and be completely free from flaws, contaminants, or defects. The piston ring portion of the turbine shaft is very hard to get clean-there are usually TWO grooves in the piston ring (see image 15a, above). If you only see one groove, good luck getting that second groove clean without marking up the piston ring portion of the turbine shaft. A Dremel tool with a wire wheel will do a pretty good job, as the shaft and wheel are usually a pretty hard

304 stainless steel, but the rule of thumb is this: if your turbine shaft's second piston ring groove cannot be cleaned, your turbine shaft is probably ruined.

Many turbo rebuild kits come with new heat shields. If yours did not, your turbo rebuild kit is a cheap piece of junk from ebay. Do not re use your heat shield unless you have to-cleaning them is a pain. The best way to go is to scrub them in degreaser with a wire brush and then hit them with a wire wheel on a dremel or in a high speed air tool. It is important to get your heat shield completely clean and grease free if you are to re-use it: a dirty heat shield may contaminate a otherwise sterile build.

Make sure ALL of your parts are clean of all debris, contaminants, old oil, solid particles, etc. A good cleaner for after you have your parts degreased is dish soap and water. Brake parts cleaner and common degreasers tend to leave a residue, and dish soap takes this residue off.   Keep in mind, a turbocharger's bearings are actually made of oil, so a contaminated oil supply means contaminated bearings, and contaminated bearings or bad oil probably ruined your turbocharger in the first place.

Re-Assembly

Now that all of your parts are clean, it is time to put them back together. It is best to take all of your clean parts into a clean room or into your house. You do not want to contaminate your clean parts with dust, dirt, or dirty motor oil.

First, re-install the clips that hold your journal bearings in place in your bearing housing. If your rebuild kit has the steel spring type inserts, have fun spending time putting those in. If your kit has internal snap rings, have fun with those, too. If your turbo has clips, it means that there is a groove that these clips fit into. The best way to install these clips is to get as much of the clip into place as possible using snap ring pliers, etc., and push the rest of the clip into place with your small straight screwdriver. Keep in mind, you CAN NOT put any tool marks on the inside of the bearing housing while putting these clips into place. Take your time, and prepare to spend a lot of time searching for the clips after they go flying or after you have to shake them loose from your bearing housing. Make sure that the clips go back into the housing after this happens are as clean as possible.

After your clips are in, or if you don't have any clips at all, it is time to insert ONE journal bearing. Put a small amount of oil into the bearing housing bore where the bearing will be inserted, and cover the new journal bearing with fresh clean oil. Put your journal bearing into the turbine side of the bearing housing FIRST. If your journal bearing is secured by a second clip, insert that clip now.

Now insert your piston ring onto the turbine shaft. DO NOT force the piston ring apart in order to get it to fit-the piston ring must have a certain gap when compressed, so you can not use piston ring tools for this operation. These rings can be fragile and very inflexible-they will not go back into their desired dimension if they are expanded with a tool. Simply work the ring into place USING NO TOOLS of any kind. Now put your heat shield in place.

At this time, coat the turbine shaft with a liberal amount of clean fresh motor oil. A clean workspace and clean hands will go a long way towards keeping dirt out of your CHRA at this point, as you may have to spend some time with the turbine shaft in order to get it into place, and you will have oily hands after trying a few times to get this to go together. The idea here is to get the piston ring on the turbine shaft to set inside of the groove of the bearing housing without the piston ring becoming damaged or coming off the piston ring groove on the turbine shaft. This can only be accomplished with finesse-if you have to force the turbine shaft into place, you are guaranteed to ruin at least the piston ring. DO NOT EVER use a hammer to get the turbine shaft into place.

The proper technique to get the turbine shaft into place is to try to compress the piston ring by putting the shaft in at a slight angle. Patience and experience are a major plus when putting the shaft into the housing-if the turbine shaft is not fully inserted into the housing, the rotating assembly/CHRA will not go together at all. Be patient and keep trying, and do not force the parts together.

After the turbine shaft is in place, do not remove it for any reason. Many times, the reason is accidental-people tend to pull the assembly apart accidentally while stacking in the rest of the bearings. The best way to assemble the rest of the CHRA is to place the bearing housing, with the turbine wheel inserted, face down on a table, to allow gravity to hold the assembly together.

So, if your turbocharger is equipped with a spring or spacer assembly between the journal bearings, insert those pieces now. Then insert the second journal bearing, after coating it with oil, onto the turbine shaft and against either the clip in the bearing housing or against the spring/spacer assembly. If your journal bearing has a second clip to hold it in place, insert that clip after inserting the journal bearing.

Now insert the thrust collar. First, coat all parts in a liberal film of oil. The thrust collar will sit on top of the journal bearing or clip, with the narrow part sticking through the thrust bearing. Now insert your new thrust bearing on top of the thrust collar. Lubricate and then re insert the O ring into the bearing housing, taking note of how the original O ring was inserted. Please take note-if your turbo was installed using thread sealer or thread lock on the screws, this thread sealer should already be installed on your new hardware. If it is not, you are up a creek-you bought a cheap ebay turbo rebuild kit. We NEVER install thread sealer on any hardware inside of a turbo, as the odds of that sealer getting into the bearing system is high. Many Chinese turbochargers fail due to excessive thread sealer/red RTV.

Assemble the thrust spacer/seal plate/oil shield assembly. Insert the thrust spacer with no piston ring through the oil shield. Now insert the piston ring onto the thrust spacer. DO NOT use any tools to expand the piston ring, you will break it. The piston ring is a special high temperature steel that is easily broken or distorted. Now insert the thrust spacer into the seal plate. Use patience and no tools: forcing the two pieces together will ruin the piece. The back of the oil shield may or may not snap into the back of the seal plate: take note of how the parts went together. They should go back together the same way.

Now coat the thrust spacer in a liberal film of oil. Insert the spacer/sealplate assembly onto the turbine shaft and into the bearing housing. The spacer/sealplate assembly will need to go down far enough so that the internal snap ring fits into the groove above the thrust spacer. The assembly typically will not go down far enough to allow the snap ring to fully seat, and many times this is a two man (or two woman) job: one person must push down on the seal plate and hold the piece down while the second person fumbles with the snap ring, shoots it across the room a few times, and finally gets it in place.

Once the snap ring is partially seated, hit the snap ring with your punch and steel hammer to force the ring in place. The snap ring must be fully seated in a way that is identical to how the ring looked before the CHRA was taken apart. Snap rings that are not totally seated will come out and ruin your entire CHRA. (see image 16c)

Image 16c: Sealplate/thrust spacer assembly inserted into bearing housing with snap ring installed and fully seated.

Now attempt to insert the compressor wheel onto the turbine shaft, after coating the shaft in a thin film of oil. If your wheel does not easily slide into place, one of two things has gone wrong. Your compressor wheel may be inappropriate for re-use because you had a major turbocharger failure. You forced the wheel off and you are being cheap and trying to re-use worn out parts. The second problem may be that you are re-using a turbine shaft and wheel that was severely blued from heat/oil starvation or you are trying to re-use a turbine shaft that is severely deflected for the same reasons. You know this because you had to force the parts apart, and you should not be re-using these parts. If none of these conditions apply, it may be possible to heat the compressor wheel up with the propane torch and to put the wheel on when it is still hot.

After the compressor wheel is in place, it is time to torque the assembly. If you are having the CHRA re-balanced, use a new shaft nut supplied in your turbo rebuild kit. If you are re-using the same compressor wheel and turbine shaft, re align the marks that you made. Your TD05/6 family turbo should be torqued to 12.2 N·m (Newton meters). Re install the O ring on the outside of the bearing housing, if equipped.

Now you are ready to install the compressor housing. Coat the O ring on the outside of the bearing housing, if equipped, with a thin layer of oil. Put the compressor housing face down on a table or a piece of wood and insert the bearing housing into the compressor housing. Note the mark you made before disassembling the turbo on the compressor cover. Align the mark with the turbocharger's feature, hopefully the oil drain flange, and either re-install the bolts or re-install the V band clamp or snap ring. If your turbocharger's CHRA has a gasket on the outside of it, it may be necessary to push the bearing housing further down into the compressor housing than the assembly wants to go. DO NOT use a hammer or any tool to accomplish this, and keep in mind, if you press the CHRA into the compressor cover so that the wheels are impacted, the chances of wheel damage are very high, which makes this entire exercise a waste of time. Be careful-many times, turbochargers that use internal snap rings are the turbos that do not want to seat fully. The proper way to seat this type of CHRA is to get the snap ring started and to fully seat the snap ring using a punch and a steel hammer.

Now place your turbine housing on a bench or table top and insert the CHRA into the turbine housing. You may notice that the CHRA does not want to easily fit into the turbine housing. This is because the turbine housing is probably not smooth and free of corrosion. Re-work the turbine housing so that the portion of the turbine housing that receives the CHRA is completely smooth and free of oxidation. You want to be able to easily insert the CHRA and you want to be able to freely rotate the CHRA in the turbine housing so that you can align the mark you made on the turbine housing with the oil return flange on the CHRA. This is more of an art and not a science.

What we do is that we get the turbine housing very close to perfect and we use a steel punch and hammer to gradually work the CHRA into place. Keep in mind, this is just like removing the CHRA from the turbine housing during the disassembly process: one bad whack with the hammer and the turbine wheel comes into contact with the turbine housing, and you are back where you started-your turbo is again ruined. It is better to rework the turbine housing so that the turbocharger cartridge fits inside the housing.

Align your marks on the turbine housing, re-install the V-band clamp and torque the clamp nut to 8.3 Newton-meters, and re-install the wastegate actuator, if equipped.

Installing the Turbo Like a Bone Head

Many customers manage to ruin new and rebuild turbos by:

- Re-using the oil supply line to the turbo

- Using a oil drain line that has a kink or hole in it

- Spinning a turbocharger up using compressed air (it is a LOT of fun, but it immediately ruins everything. Turbos need pressurized oil)

- Using tefflon thread tape, thread sealer, or silicone on the oil supply or oil drain line

- Not changing their oil before they change their turbo

- Not changing their air filter before changing the turbo

- Not priming their turbo before operation

- Putting the turbo back on an engine with a bad oil pump, a bad PCV valve, or an engine that has massive blowby past the piston rings

After installing your turbo, you must:

Use a new oil feed line. No exceptions. Oil deposits get broken loose on used oil feed lines, and these deposits will go directly to your turbo's bearings and ruin the whole thing.

Change your oil every 5,000 miles and before you put the new turbo on. We do not care if your oil change costs $500, you have to keep fresh oil in a turbo.

Change your air filter and vacuum out your air box. Cummins turbos WILL suck an entire dirty filter into the compressor side and take out your whole engine. ONE piece of dirt will eat a turbo's wheels.

Disconnect your fuel pump after installing your turbo and crank your engine until the oil pressure light goes out. Your turbo must have pressurized oil. All the time.

Conclusion

Turbochargers are expensive, finicky pieces of high-speed equipment. They cannot operate in out of spec conditions, and they must be in balance at all times. Rebuilding a turbocharger is a difficult job that can be performed under certain conditions by normal people, but the outcome of a questionable rebuild may not be known unless a turbocharger is placed on a balancer after rebuild. Out of spec turbos may operate for prolonged periods of time, and an out of spec improperly rebuilt turbocharger may not immediately fail, but it will never perform properly. There are dozens of ways to improperly rebuild a turbocharger, and this guide will hopefully offer some guidance in order to avoid doing things wrong.

The crucial step in rebuilding a turbocharger is to always check the balance of the CHRA. This check will show problems in assembly, machining, and balance, and the operator of a turbocharger balancer will be able to attempt to correct problems before CHRA are put into service. Unfortunately, a used balancer typically costs around $10,000, so home balancing is not an option.

We recommend sending any rebuild CHRA to a turbocharger shop that runs a balancer: every manufacturer of turbochargers, even Chinese manufacturers, checks and corrects balance before releasing CHRA for service as a means of quality control. If a diesel shop that rebuilds turbos does not have a balancer, they should not rebuild. Find a turbo shop that runs a balancer, and get your turbo balanced before it enters service.

Ebay Buying Guide for Turbocharger Parts

Ebay has become a major marketplace for turbocharger parts and turbochargers, but Ebay has devolved from a legitimate place to buy turbos into a dumping ground for questionable aftermarket parts from China. Without some simple rules of thumb, though, you're going to have a bad time buying turbocharger parts on Ebay.

In 2004, when we started selling on Ebay, almost all of the turbos and parts available were legitimate. There were some Chinese turbos, but the Chinese turbo rebuild kits did not yet exist on Ebay. Only parts manufactured by Garrett, Mitsubishi, Mitsubishi, KKK, and IHI were available through legitimate dealers, and aftermarket distributors kept tight control on their quality and lines of supply. In 2012, the situation has completely changed.

Nearly every turbocharger part for sale on Ebay is made in China. There is a lot of talk online, in enthusiast forums, that this is no big deal: everything is made in China, companies like Garrett make turbos in China, so these parts must be ok. The problem with this is that the people making these arguments do not work in the turbocharger industry. Yes, many good companies make parts in China. But these companies own their own factories, and these companies DO NOT allow their branded parts outside of their lines of supply. Chinese parts that are made for a company like Mitsubishi stay in the Chinese market. They never leave China.

The Chinese marketplace is a very large marketplace, second only to the United States, and the demand for replacement turbochargers in this market is very strong. Companies in China have started up just to meet this demand, and many more companies have started up just to sell aftermarket turbocharger parts. Because the demand is so large, unqualified start up companies will decide one day to start mass producing bearings. Another company will buy these bearings, sight unseen, in bulk, and flood the market with these parts. No one knows why the bearings have a certain design, no one knows what the engineering tolerances are or why they exist, but everyone knows that a certain bearing will sell in the hundreds of millions every year. The same thing happens for parts like turbine wheels, CHRA, and full turbos.

How do we know? We have been to China, and we have ordered three CHRA and a total of 40 turbos from different manufacturers there. The conditions in the factory should have prevented us from buying, but because we bought a new suit and an expensive plane ticket, we figured it was a good idea to keep losing money, so we ignored the fact that the machinist finishing the turbine wheels was working next to some forklifts and didn't have any sleeves on his filthy shirt.

Two CHRA that showed up were not actually the right parts, even though we ordered using part numbers. One of the CHRA's turbine wheels was made of mild steel instead of aerospace Inconel 713-it would have rusted through or disintegrated over time. One of the CHRA was actually not that bad, and was the right part number. The turbos that were placed in service had a 35% failure rate. Compressor wheels exploded, bearings failed, and there were failures because v band clamps were not installed correctly. We determined that China was a viable source for parts, but every piece of every turbo would have to be examined, measured, and assembled by us. After that, entire shipments would show up with 80-90% of the parts being out of spec. Why does this matter?

All of the parts seemed fine to the eye. They looked fine. Because they were designed to fool the eye, like a counterfeit handbag. If you examine a real designer purse using a micrometer, or even a ruler, and then examine a counterfeit copy in the same way, you will notice that none of the dimensions are exactly right. An inch here, a mm there on a purse won't matter that much, but turbocharger parts, real ones, have tolerances of microns. A company like Garrett does not insist on these kind of specs because they really like order, they do this because they know that their parts must be perfect if they are going to put millions of one part in service in one year and remain in business. Garrett does quality control over and over and over on their parts, but Chinese companies do it one or two times: the company that makes the bearings is trusted to make bearings to spec, and then another company will check the balance of a assembled turbo or CHRA.

A Chinese sales company will sell a few hundred, or even a thousand, turbos or bearings on ebay in a year, so a failure rate of 40% on parts marked up 5000% will not ruin them. These companies know, too, that their low price point lowers expectations: a turbocharger failure in a $200 turbo may not even result in a refund.

We purchased an aftermarket, Japanese-sounding branded bearing housing, compressor housing, and turbine housing from a company that specializes in TD05/6 family Mitsubishi style turbochargers on Ebay. This company claims that their parts are "authentic," and even some of the parts ship from Japan (and some ship from Taiwan). We stayed away from their turbine shafts, as another shop told us that these Japanese sounding turbine shafts were not even polished to a mirror finish. When we put the assembly together, the compressor cover didn't exactly fit into the bearing housing, so the snap ring did not seat all the way. It looked like it was half way in place, but it seemed secure. Because we only deal with quality parts, we didn't recognize this as a major problem. We built and balanced the CHRA ourselves, so a snap ring being secure but not completely seated seemed like a minor problem. Until the snap ring popped out of place entirely and the compressor cover came off. On a running engine.

Ebay has a lot of quality parts and brands, and it has a lot of Chinese garbage turbos and parts, too. Many companies take great pains to hide where their parts come from, and some companies illegally use other established trademarks and logos to hide the fact that their turbochargers and parts are just Chinese. Rebranding junk parts is one common trick, using Japanese sounding names. Another trick is to claim that the seller is the manufacturer of the turbocharger or any of its parts. If you are not careful, you will believe that parts being marketed as the same as the real are the real thing unless you ask questions.

You, the Ebay buyer, can get to the bottom of things by just asking who makes the parts you are buying and where the parts are made. The only companies that should be manufacturing turbos are Garrett, Mitsubishi, KKK, IHI, and Borg-Warner. If you find out that the parts you are buying are made in China, ask yourself a simple question: is it worth $100 to get quality bearings? Does it make sense to save $50 on a turbo rebuild kit if the kit is a total piece of garbage? Chinese bearings, for our company, may cost about $5 for a complete set if we wanted them. We don't buy them because we don't have the resources to inspect thousands of bearings, hoping to weed out the ones that are bad. We pay companies like Garrett to do that for us because we know that every part that shows up is perfect. Assume that every part for sale on Ebay is made in China and weigh your decision accordingly.

Made in the USA
Monee, IL
22 December 2024

75263795R00050